Person
and
Institution

Person
and
Institution

JOHN P. SISK, *1914-*

FIDES PUBLISHERS, INC.
NOTRE DAME, INDIANA

© Copyright: 1970,
FIDES PUBLISHERS, INC., NOTRE DAME, INDIANA

Library of Congress Catalog Card Number: 73-79245
Standard Book Number: 8190-0433-2

Preface

This book grew out of my effort to understand the relationship between person and institution, particularly when the person is a post-Vatican II Christian and the institution is the Church. The question of this relationship has in fact been made especially urgent by the Council, one of the apparent side-effects of which has been to widen the gap between person and institution. Indeed, the very notion of renewal implies that very critical distance between person and institution out of which comes an awareness of the need of renewal. It follows that while the prospect of renewal may be exhilarating, the experienced fact of it will at times be painful and even frightening. And of course, renewal can be very frustrating since the act of renewing discovers fresh evidence of the need of renewal. Renewal, in other words, functions like a medium of communication.

Nothing more complicates man's efforts at renewal than his uncertainty about how he relates to his institutions, since this is ultimately an uncertainty about his own nature. For reasons intricately involved with the development of the modern world, our habit is to think and speak of institutions as naturally hostile to persons, so that true personhood seems to involve utter separation from their inhibiting and corrupting powers. In this view, institutional relationships, if they cannot be entirely avoided, must be guarded and suspicious, as if one were for the time being forced to exist next door to a sworn enemy. So our dreams of personal liberation tend to be visions of de-institutionalized conditions. They image states of ideal harmony quite opposite to the traditional picture of the institution (especially the Church) as both the embodiment and agent of harmony among individuals.

This book is grounded on the conviction that the polarization of person and institution—as if the institution were a fundamentally alien thing "out there" imposed upon man by some hostile force—is a prime source of the confusion and suffering of post-Vatican II Christians. Whether one is speaking of the secular or sacred domain, personal life is institutional life; institutionalization is a dimension of humanization. But a Christian may only half believe this, in which case his efforts to reform the institutions that structure his religious life are constantly undercut by a modern suspicion (often masked as an enthusiastic personalism) that the needs of spirit are incompatible with institutional life. This suspicion is aggravated by the communication media, which are at least as well adapted to discovering corruption in institutions as they are to any other purpose.

In a very real sense, then, the problem of person and institution is both a problem of communication and a problem of corruption. Corruption never ceases to be a problem, but it is special kind of problem in an age convinced that corruption is a special characteristic of institutions, and that if it can be eliminated from institutions (or eliminated with institutions) virtue will at last have a chance. Hence we make the institution a scapegoat for our own corruption and the corruption of the institution our justification for those all-or-nothing crusades in which virtue itself becomes a tyranny even more constricting than the institution it sets out to correct or remove. And tyrannous virtue, by staking all on a passionately limited point of view, fails as charity and fails as communication theory.

It seemed to me in the beginning that I might say all this in a single essay—at least in a synoptic way. Instead I found myself writing an integrated series of five essays, each of which after the first being made necessary because of the position at which the previous one had arrived. However, I have no sense of having closed the circle. A subject of this complexity is without end, like the subject of the meaning of *Hamlet*. One might well conclude it as Lawrence Durrell does his *Alexandria Quartet:* with an appendix in which one lists "workpoints" that might be further explored. In this case, one of such workpoints might be the effect that the modern myth of discontinuity (the belief in the possibility of an utterly fresh start) has had on our thinking about the person-institution relationship. Another might be the influence of the utopian tradition on this relationship, particularly in view of the combination in this tradition of a self-defeating idealism with an antipersonal fear of nonconformity—the historical result of which combination has been that frightful mega-institution, the totalitarian state. Still another might be the role that architectural metaphors, with their tendency to identify institutions with their visible forms, have played in our thinking about institutional reforms. Indeed, an understanding of the relationship between personhood and institutional life is so vital to an understanding of the human condition that it is hard to imagine an end to such a list.

The first four chapters of this book appeared originally as separate essays in *The National Catholic Reporter*. I wish to thank the publishers for permission to reprint this material. The passage of time has made it necessary to revise the first three essays, though I have not attempted to alter them in any basic way. I am also grateful to the Fides editors for having made it possible for me to attend the Fides Forum at Notre Dame University in December of 1967. The papers and discussions at this Forum proved to be of great value to me when I came to write the final two chapters.

Gonzaga University
November, 1969

The evils of the church that now is are manifest. The question returns, What shall we do? I confess, all attempts to project and establish a Cultus with new rites and forms, seem to me vain. All attempts to contrive a system are as cold as the new worship introduced by the French to the goddess of Reason—today, pasteboard and filagree, and ending tomorrow in madness and murder. Rather let the breath of new life be breathed by you through the forms already existing. For if once you are alive, you shall find they shall become plastic and new.

RALPH WALDO EMERSON
"The Divinity School Address"

Contents

xiii

1
Mater as Magistra

In the 1965 McGeary Foundation Lecture at Mundelein College, Gregory Baum, O.S.A., gave as the reason for the papacy's nineteenth century condemnation of the doctrine of religious liberty the fact that "the people who then defended it tended to deny that man was bound by any norm of truth at all." However, he pointed out, contemporary Catholic thought "has clearly separated the idea of religious liberty from the false foundation proposed in the last century; it has convincingly grounded it on the dignity of the human person." Here, said Father Baum, we have "an example of where a deeper appreciation of personhood as well as the evolution of society has modified the Church's position on a crucial question of man's moral life."

1

Indeed, one who has not heard the accents of that teaching voice in the Church that seeks to develop personhood has missed one of the most significant expressions of the modern Catholic spirit. But the Church, like any institution that expresses a world view in competition with other world views, teaches in many ways and with more than one voice. To those who did not already know it, the Council has made it clear that there is a teaching voice in the Church that does not favor the development of personhood. This teaching voice is an expression of the process of the Church, the verbal counterpart to something in its style and structure that tends to thwart efforts to release the person to his full Christian potential—and this in spite of the Church's historical concern for the individual soul, without which there would be no ground for the development of personhood.

All institutions in their style and structure constitute a teaching voice, the rhetoric of which is no less persuasive because it is nonverbal. Ideally, of course, style, structure and process simply repeat in another mode the values and objectives the institution is verbally committed to, so that substantially it speaks with a single voice. The institution, like the poem, aspires to a condition in which theme, structure and style are integral, in which its meaning is a function of its whole being. But the poem, though it may also suffer from a conflict of verbal and nonverbal voices, is much more likely to approach this ideal than an institution is. Indeed, the poem, or work of art, can be just as dangerous a model for institution formation as for character formation. For the poem having been made an integrated whole has come to the end of its process, whereas an institution is always in process and is fortunate to have its poem-like moments—and these only because the conflict of voices in it appears momentarily to have ceased or has been forcibly suppressed.

Obviously we are not living in such a moment. The new teaching voice in the Church (and its counterparts in liturgy and general Church style) conflicts in its championship of personhood with an older teaching voice and its institutional counterparts. It is not correct to say that this older voice is simply against the person, for it is expressed within and qualified by an institution that is also the repository of values indispensable to the realization of personhood. It is a traditional voice but it does not gather to itself all the tradition, however useful it may be for tactical purposes to give the impression that it does. For the new voice claims not to have brought something foreign into the Church but to have articulated and put fresh emphasis on something that was already there.

The extent to which it was already there is made brilliantly clear in the "Fortunata" section of Erich Auerbach's *Mimesis,* where St. Mark's account of Peter's denial of Christ is shown to violate (of course not consciously) the classic rule of the differentiation of styles. It is not hard to draw from Auerbach's study of this violation the conclusion that the ground for our sense of the person is the New Testament. For left to its own devices, classical rhetoric, with its tendency to "view from above" the humble quotidian realities of life and to deny to them any stylistic dignity or lasting worth, would scarcely have arrived at the person. In the classical world the lowly fisherman belonged in idyl or farce; he could never have been the focus of tragedy or the subject of a salvation story meaningful to all men.

Nevertheless, Church style and structure as we know them have been determined in great part by the historical incidence of heresy, schism and reformation, and by the socio-political habits of the classical and medieval periods. One result has been a ghetto atmosphere and a ghetto emphasis on solidarity against the enemy outside. The accent has been on the rights of authority to rule and be obeyed. Church style and structure, quite understandably then, teach the importance of subordinating the individual, not only in the interest of his enriching participation in the community of believers, but in the interest of the operating needs of an institution inclined for historical reasons to be suspicious of him. Church style, structure and process therefore point up the timeless, the eternal, the unchanging, the general, against the threats of controversy, passion and the world. Because of its past it remains strongly classical, still wistfully attached to the stable, controllable (and controlling) Latin over the shifting and unpredictable vernacular. Thus it has both a rhetorical and linguistic bias against its own radical potential for fostering personhood.

To say that the institutional habit of the Church is to look upon controversy as a threat is not to say, however, that it is inclined to avoid controversy. With its highly rhetorical organization it is controversy-prone. But controversy describes the relationship that exists between the institution and its enemies. Controversy means the questioning or nonacceptance of authority and implies the threat of schism or heresy. Controversy in this context tends to cover all differences of interpretation or opinion, all attempts at criticism or dialogue. Its defining opposite is dogmatic unanimity and a suppression of the merely personal in the body of the faithful. The merely personal means opinion, and where there is opinion there is always the threat of controversy. To pay serious attention to personhood, then, is to cater to a potential disrupter of harmony.

The older voice in the Church is not only deficient in the techniques necessary to enter into dialogue with the person, but its style impedes the development of such techniques. Whatever its potential for encouraging personhood, it is organized to pass orders down a chain of command, as if from a king through a hierarchy of vassals to peasants, addressing itself not to individual persons but to Christian man. Its organizational concern is with the universal, with what men have in common. One of the natural results of its process is the company Catholic, the man of uncritical allegiance whose emotional attachment to the Church is often less an expression of religious awareness than an attachment to a ritualized principle of order. For such a one, the controversial is nothing more than a willful assertion of the personal, and almost by definition immoral. The new voice and the new ways in the Church, though derived from its living tradition, are likely to be profoundly disturbing to him, particularly when they involve a conflict among authorities.

Like all highly complex organizations, the Church has a strong tendency to use the efficiency of the established chain of command as an index to its general moral well-being. If the directives are going through and are being obediently acted on, all is well. The smooth functioning of the process justifies the institution in terms of its overall objectives. Thus we have what might be called the operational fallacy: what runs well must be running in the right direction. All organizations tend to teach this fallacy, not formally but in the very act of existing, which is only to say that they tend to teach their own processes. An institution in a state of decadence teaches little else, since it has ceased to be vitally concerned with anything as much as it is concerned with its own continued existence. An organization of any complexity therefore depends on pressure from inspectors, eccentrics, devil's advocates, saints and even heretics to keep it from confusing its objectives with its own process.

All other things being equal, then, the ability to tolerate and even benefit from difference of opinion, and therefore from controversy, is an index to the health of an organization. In a pluralist world it is especially important that a religious institution not only be at ease in controversy but that it teach its members how to handle themselves in controversial situations. They must be further taught to distinguish between controversy that aims at successful defense of an unquestioned position and controversy aimed at discovering the truth. To teach them otherwise is to teach the habits of the unexamined life and the fear of their own persons.

The wariness about passion works to the same end. Inevitably, among the most controversial subjects in the Church at the present time are those relating to sex and marriage. All institutions (even bawdy houses) have a protective fear of passion, and of sex in particular—sex with its tendency to abstract the individual out of the normal orbit of his existence, to cancel all claims of a higher allegiance as soon as it seems that the claims of sex cannot be reconciled with it. Orwell and Huxley in

1984 and *Brave New World* have clearly dramatized the radical conflict between the state and sex and the extent to which the state's efforts to control sex can be an effort to suppress the person. From the point of view of those at the centers of power, persons in their sexual capacity dramatize not only the touchy relationship between sex and authority but the precarious nature of all human management of power. But this is true for the individual as well, particularly in a society traditionally inclined to disjoin reason and passion; he must live with the ticking bomb of his own passions, and so is never entirely unhappy to see his fear protectively institutionalized in state of Church.

The Church shares the state's fears of passion and sex but has its special fears since it considers sex in a context that has a moral and theological dimension. It has the great practical advantage over the state in that it can sacramentalize sex in marriage. It is therefore doctrinally committed to a positive and creative attitude towards sex, a fact of the greatest importance to the development of personhood in Western civilization.

At the same time, the Church is an institution in which divine grace acts through human instruments in particular times and places. Its attitudes towards passion and sex have been colored by the pagan world—not only by the traumatic experience of pagan sensuality in the decaying Roman world but by the Platonism and stoicism that reinforced its own tendencies to melodramatize the disjunction between body and soul, passion and reason. Hence the strong tendency in the Church to speak of body-soul and passion-reason relations in terms of military combat. Body and passion are the enemy, conspiring against soul and reason; one is urged to eternal vigilance against them; one fights them to subdue them. Sex then tends to be imbedded in a context of eternal hazard.

The official theory of these relationships is of course a good deal more refined and shaded than this; indeed, it would have to be to avoid heresy. However, it is not so much the theory that directly affects living Christians as the public rhetoric, schematized and simplified for hortatory and didactic purposes and hyperbolized to counter the anticipated resistance of real or imagined opposition. Insofar as this rhetorical tradition is operative it is a formidable obstacle to Christian marriage, which then tends to be a union founded not on respect for but fear of the body, a seedbed not for personhood but neurosis.

The traditional tendency to separate reason from passion, which results in a denigration of the affective and imaginative in man's nature, is not only in effect a way of dividing the person against himself and so reducing him as a menace to authority, but is also a way of separating the artist from the Church. The tension between the artist and the Church is in part the result of commitments that tend to be absolute, but that tension is aggravated by the fact that in style, structure and process the Church is strongly oriented to a pre-Romantic world view in which the artist was thought of as a normative reflector of a relatively stable and rationally ordered universe—a universe that could be quite adequately articulated by (as it was indeed in part created by) classical rhetoric.

But the Romantic artist was projective rather than imitative, committed to a personal and private vision, to organicism, and process. As such he was a striking manifestation of modern man's effort to tear himself loose from the encompassing social mass and become, at the expense of whatever agonies and confusions, more truly a person. He became the person intensified and of necessity an alienated man, dangerously inclined to let the image he could create become his god. Kings and prelates continued to give him lip-service, remembering the days when he was a valuable asset, but tended more and more to see him as the liberator of subversive forces that society had traditionally dedicated itself to keeping in check. If he stayed in the Church he tended to find himself torn between two masters (the tension was of course sometimes good for him). He was the living and highly critical presence of what the future promised to be, as disruptive of normal operations as the mystic or the saint, both of whom he resembled in important ways. He was passional man cut loose from the guiding reins; he aroused fears that the reins themselves were defective.

But the Church's uneasiness with passion and sex is only an aspect of its opposition to the world. Clearly, the Christ-oriented man must resist the world insofar as it is the order of time and change manifesting itself as desacralized or as radically hostile to the sacred (the human condition conceived of as simply one damned thing after another, as Aldous Huxley once put it). But in the heat and exigency of day-to-day hortatory polemics the world long ago tended to become the temporal, material order in its capacity to inspire human interest and engagement. Though this extension of the term tended to make St. Stylites' pillar the Great Good Place, it was in one sense a clear gain: it satisfied the practical need to reduce the complex problem of the Christian's location in time and change to a disjunctive clarity.

This rhetorical simplification of a crucial term (understandable given the context in which the Church has at times found itself) made it highly unlikely that Teilhard's question would be asked: "Why should there not be men vowed to the task of exemplifying, by their lives, the general sanctification of human endeavor?" Teilhard knew that there have always been such men and that there has always been a teaching voice in the Church to support them, however hard it might have been over long periods of time to hear it. However, his question alludes to that other voice, essentialist and wary of time and change, that so powerfully uses the teaching example of the saints to suggest that safety lies only in extreme disengagement from human endeavors. Caught between these voices, the post-Reformation Catholic has too often suffered that "paralyzing perplexity" and "veritable spiritual dualism" about which Teilhard speaks in *The Divine Milieu*.

To be so perplexed about one's place in the world and about one's natural impulses to engage himself in the human effort is to doubt one's value as a person. To despise the world in the wrong sense is to despise oneself, for to despise the world is to despise time and change, the necessary dimensions of personal development. To put it another way, Manichaeism, with its conviction that the world cannot be redeemed, is the occupational hazard of Christianity. The hazard is not lessened by the otherwise valuable heritage of classical rhetoric in the style and structure of the Church: specifically, by its tendency to define by contrast; to make sharp disjunctions in the interest of polemical efficiency; to think of communication as persuasion rather than dialogue; to "fix" reality in water-tight definitions; to look with suspicion upon that which resists clear subordination; to stand cautiously away from the dense complexity of life in order to see it in terms of large manageable categories.

The political consequences of the Church's "otherworldly" teaching voice, with its tendency to counsel disengagement from the time- and change-bound world, have been clear enough. Significant numbers of the hierarchy and laity have stayed outside of, looked with apprehension on or opposed the great social and political movements of the past hundred years because they have been unable to dissociate them from evils they have felt bound to oppose. Those who were able to make the dissociation had to do so in the face of strong institutional bias against changes that threatened what the late Thomas Merton has called the "assumption that medieval Christianity was a unique and timeless norm which we must work to reestablish."

The teaching voice in the Church that accepts this norm is not likely to argue explicitly for it; it rather adheres to the institutional correlatives of this norm in the Church's style, structure and process. This adherence makes inevitable a skepticism about some of the most important efforts to alleviate the human condition and an apprehension about some of the most promising efforts to liberate the person from those forces that have traditionally kept him docile before authority and inclined to accept without question, as part of God's plan, whatever state he found himself in.

The Council did not change all this. Its consensus on freedom of conscience, on the Jews, on ecumenicism, on changes in the liturgy (especially the use of the vernacular), was clearly a stand favorable to the person as against an older emphasis on his beneficient submersion in the interest of institutional needs. But the Council also forced the older teaching voice in the Church to sharpen its defenses. However the so-called conservative party might have appeared to be outnumbered, it had the immense advantage of being identified with what for a long time has been taken to be the only authentic voice of the Church to which all accommodations must be made. As the Monsignor Illich affair made clear, it is reluctant to give up this advantage.

But it cannot press this advantage without benefiting the person. The Council in its day-to-day function asserted the extent to which the voice of the Church is now, as to one degree or another it has always been, a dialectic of voices, unified by a common body of dogma and a common commitment of faith, engaged with one another in an effort to make ever more manifest the full implications of Christ's gospel. The Council demonstrates the paradox that the protection of the body of faith depends on such a continuing dialectic of discovery in time. And in proportion as the Council was a dramatic instance of such an effort it was on the side of personhood even in those moments when its apparent thrust was against personhood. In its style, structure and process it encouraged the individual Christian to reexamine honestly his own commitment to Christ through the Church.

In the meantime, all teaching voices in the Church have at least one urgent practical reason for not standing against the person, and that is the ease with which the Church is made the scapegoat, not only for abuses of authority everywhere, but for all manner of personal failures to come to terms with authority in any context whatever. This is apparent in much of the over-heated criticism of Church tradition, the very immoderation of which suggests that its real relevance is to unstated issues. Some of this criticism implies as an ideal a utopian disjunction of personhood and authority that ignores the realities of time and change just as vigorously as does the teaching voice it objects to.

It is a dangerous naivete, then, to think that all attacks on Church tradition are authentic strikes for personhood. The Church remains, for whatever lack of agreement among its teaching voices, the hope of the person. This is why those who are for the person should hope not that the new voice triumphantly sweep all before it, and so become in time an entrenched old voice, but that all voices remain in open and charitable contention. The person stands to gain as long as the dialogue continues; what is against him is monologue.

2
Sweet Dream of Harmony

It is as safe these days to be for harmony as it is to be against sin or communism. Thus Msgr. William L. Doty, writing in *America* (April 9, 1966) on "Controversy Within the Church," could surely feel uncontroversial in stating that "the spirit of dialogue cannot be successfully promoted without the support of prayer, and particularly liturgical prayer, for harmony within the Church." Who in these often painfully inharmonious times would refuse to join in such prayer? But suppose our very preoccupation with harmony and the unexamined assumptions that support it themselves impede the spirit of dialogue?

Some years ago Saul Steinberg made such a preoccupation the subject of a *New Yorker* cover

(January 17, 1959). In this satiric vision semantics has disposed of unemployment and statistics has cured inflation; symbolic figures shaking hands represent the reconciliation of Uncle Sam and Uncle Tom, Labor and Leisure, Vice and Virtue, Art and Industry, Science and Commerce; Prosperity, a portly top-hatted figure bracketed between Santa Claus and Sigmund Freud, stands high on a pedestal with links of a broken chain hanging triumphantly from each wrist. Dialogue, controversy, friction—all are over. Indeed—for this is the logic of such a vision—time itself is over and nothing more, not even prosperity, can happen, and the artist very appropriately arranges his statement as an elaborate public monument.

Steinberg's cover mocks the sweet dream of harmony to which all institutions, sacred as well as secular, attempt to give dramatic form. The attempt is inseparable from their attempt to operate efficiently. Institutions strive to establish themselves as metaphors of harmony, not only to secure themselves but in response to public demand for such metaphors. The faith they inspire in men is an important factor in maintaining such harmony as there is in human affairs. This is why public relations departments are necessities, not luxuries: they build internal morale, for executives, rulers and hierarchies can stand very little inharmonious reality.

A history of the great models of harmony would

probably come close to being a history of civilization. Let us simply note here that throughout most of western civilization one of the most compelling models was the universe itself, whether conceived of as a chain of being, a grand cosmic dance or an integrated arrangement of correspondences. It gave expression to the harmony that "is in immortal souls," as Lorenzo tells Jessica in a beautiful passage in *The Merchant of Venice*. As God's own work of art, it was the ultimate organizing sanction for the individual and for human affairs generally. Therefore Lorenzo can say that the man who

> . . . hath no music in himself,
> Nor is not moved with concord of sweet sounds,
> Is fit for treasons, stratagems and spoils;
> The motions of his spirit are dull as night,
> And his affections dark as Erebus.
> Let no such man be trusted.

Scientists like Galileo or political theorists like Machiavelli who tampered with this concord of sweet sounds were to be distrusted equally with heretics, and were often grouped with them as rejectors of the Grand Harmonizer himself.

Events since Vatican II have made it clear how committed the Church still is to a model of harmony received from the classical and medieval world, and the extent to which individual Catholics are therefore still determined by a relatively static and archaic picture of the universe, which consciously they must reject. Emotionally, they are still nervous about Galileo, who in his effect on the grand model of traditional Christian harmony becomes a contemporary of Teilhard or Archbishop Thomas D. Roberts.

Institutions are by nature conservative, which means that they have a built-in tendency to become museums of outmoded harmonic systems. The further they are removed in time from their models of harmony the more they tend to idealize them, especially if there is a serious threat from competing models. If the pressure of this competition is great enough the idealization verges on sheer creation. Thus the historian C. Vann Woodward shows us that complex institution, the American South, creating out of its dialectic need a vision of post-Civil War interracial harmony that depended upon a highly selective and superficial organization of the facts of history. How persuasive that vision of harmony still is in some quarters can be seen in Birchite Robert Welch's reference to the Jim Crow era as one that included only "a very, very tiny amount of injustice."

Similarly, Vatican II, and the forces of renewal which it released into the Christian world, are in great part responsible for the present idealization of the old pre-Council harmony, against which Catholics like the late Evelyn Waugh measure the post-Council discords. It is apparent that to many Catholics, both lay and clerical, the novelties and consequent controversies of the past few years have had the effect of discovering and highlighting for them what appears to be the history of a centuries-long harmonious enterprise that is now threatened on every hand. Even many progressives, who entered enthusiastically into the spirit of renewal, are nervous, affected as they are bound to be by the vision of a traditional harmony and unable to imagine the Church without it.

That there is considerable disparity between this vision and the historical Church, books like John T. Noonan's *Contraception* make clear enough. The vision of the Church Harmonious is just that—a vision, a model against which it defines itself. Christians use that model much as men in a state of technological and civilized complexity use the model of a harmonious nature as a measure of the failures of civilization. Both the vision of nature and the vision of the Church Harmonious are expressions of man's pastoral impulse towards a condition of clarity, simplicity and ideal concord.

Such models, however, are anything but simple in their effects. In so far as they are means by which man exercises control over himself and his environment, they have a creative aspect: they are, that is, very real factors in such harmony and order as exist. To tamper with them, or with the institutions that claim to embody them, can have disordering consequences. Henry Adams gives us in *The Education of Henry Adams* a classic example of the sense of disorder that men experience when science tampers with the traditional model of nature—"this Eden of their own invention," as he puts it. The Jim Crow South, like the pre-Council Church, had a degree of order and tranquility now conspicuously missing from it. Having established themselves as metaphors of harmony, each was a powerful source of order in the lives of their faithful.

But in the very act of existing such metaphors tend to be disjunctive: their dramatic implication is that the only alternative is a state of discord and disorder. For Dostoevsky's Grand Inquisitor in *The Brothers Karamazov,* for instance, this state is the only alternative to the "one unanimous and harmonious ant-heap" for which all men crave. But in so far as changing conditions, discoveries or fresh insights make it apparent that this disjunction is wrong, these metaphoric embodiments of harmony are demoralizing.

Henry Adams' demoralization can be seen not only in his expressed disillusions with the "new multiverse" but in his polarization of Virgin and Dynamo and in his idealization of Amiens cathedral, that definition-by-contrast which determines his view of the multiverse. The demoralization of the South can be seen not only in the fanatic defenders of an irrelevant dream of harmony but also in those who, having lost faith in the dream, have nothing to put in its place—which is exactly the condition the dream itself warned them against.

We see similar signs of demoralization among Catholics now: on the one hand the intransigent defenders of the old harmonic system, on the other hand the disillusioned and the disaffected. Both are victims of the sweet dream of harmony—dancers who having learned to move to one tempo only are thrown into confusion when it unexpectedly changes.

It is the unexpected and unpredictable that disturb traditional models of harmony; and no doubt part of their function is to protect society from the full impact of an unpredictability it cannot contend with, or does not wish to contend with. Their common denominator then has been the cliche, with its assertion of ideal predictability. "The prevalence of cliches," says Norbert Wiener, "is no accident, but inherent in the nature of information." Elsewhere in the same work (*The Human Use of Human Beings*) he remarks that "the more probable the message, the less information it gives. Cliches, for example, are less illuminating than great poems." But at any given moment the likely thing is that society will be (as the Grand Inquisitor knows) more interested in order and harmony than in new information and illumination. In fact, society's customary protective procedure is to turn its great poems into cliches lest they convey more information than it can handle. In the same way the Church's traditional image of itself as a grand metaphor of harmony functions like a cliche-poem that obscures valuable elements in its own tradition, which if acknowledged would tend to disturb that image.

The cliche is a microcosmic institution with the institution's passion to conserve. Its great attraction is its promise to store information so that it does not depreciate in value. In a changing world, Wiener points out, this is a false promise. One might anthropomorphize the cliche and say that it knows this very well and therefore tries to keep change from happening, or at least to keep it from being recognized as a fact of the first order of importance. Therefore the cliche-structured mind is likely to miss what anthropologist Loren Eiseley calls the "strange unexpectedness" that lingers about our twentieth century world (*The American Scholar*, Summer, 1966).

The unexpectedness is what one is confronted with once he has been forced to question the grand models of harmony that control his world. Then perhaps one begins to suspect that, as Professor Eiseley says (and as the Steinberg cover agrees), "order, in a human sense, is at least partially an illusion." But this discovery is negative and sterile unless one goes beyond this point to discover that order in the human sense is also partially a creation that functions like an illusion in proportion as it is believed to be permanently valid.

The grand models of harmony in our history, which were conceived to be permanently valid, induced one to believe that problems could be permanently solved. In effect this has meant that conditions subsequently proven to be problems—slavery, political inequality, the economic distance between the rich few and the poor masses, the inferior status of women, the subordination of the person to institutional needs—were accepted as necessary aspects of order. But to question the ordered structure is to discover the hidden problems—and, as we have learned in our own time, to solve the problems in an effort to reestablish harmony is only to create more problems which disrupt it.

We can see the analogue of all this in the Church. Bemused by its own image as a metaphor of harmony, it solved too many problems by accepting them as necessary conditions of its harmonic system. The ironic thing is the extent to which many Catholics have been able to acknowledge the problems without learning the lesson: who, for instance, are so often disconcerted to discover that welcome changes in the liturgy or in the relationship between authority and the individual's conscience do not result in a terminal and unproblematic state of affairs. Progressive or liberal Catholics, it would seem, are as likely as conservatives to expect permanent solutions; they simply want to replace one sweet dream of harmony with another shaped more to their taste. They apparently find Professor Eiseley's "strange unexpectedness" as uncongenial as the old restrictive harmony.

But they are no different from men generally, who would like to see this special mark of our time itself approached as a problem to be permanently solved. It is this realization that leads the economist Robert Heilbroner to speak of the future of capitalism in these terms (*Commentary*, April, 1966):

> The key word of the new society is apt to be *control*. Not alone economic affairs (which should become of secondary importance), but the numbers and location of the population and its genetic quality, the manner of social domestication of children, the choice of life-work—even the very duration of life itself—are all apt to become subjects for scientific investigation and direction.

Professor Heilbroner is outlining here a technological dream of harmony that has obvious affinities with the "utopias" depicted by Aldous Huxley and George Orwell. The prospect makes him uneasy: "There lurks a dangerous collectivist tinge in the prospect of controls designed for the enlargement of man but inherently capable of his confinement as well." The sweet dream of harmony is always a cybernetic dream, an idyl of control in which confinement is made to appear as enlargement. This, I take it, is the significance of the broken chain in the Steinberg cover. If men are to be confined in the world of the new capitalism their confinement will be in the interest of one more sweet dream of harmony, and the victim— even the enemy—will be, as usual, the person.

In such a state of affairs (not entirely strange to us now) the Church can be a powerful champion of the person, but only if it does not offer to save him by proposing to absorb him into another and conflicting harmonic system. The Church needs to recognize its own inherent vitality and liberality: its dependence on loyal opposition, on divergent views engaged with one another in particular times and places, over issues often doubtful and ambiguous, in a continuing effort to discover its own meaning. It needs to recognize that we may have at least as much reason to be scandalized at the means by which harmony is achieved as by those criticisms and interpretations that result in disharmony. It needs to recognize, in other words, that it shares with all institutions a certain tendency to applaud the Grand Inquisitor.

What Professor Noonan's book, or any good history of the Church, makes clear is the extent to which the actual existence of the Church has been disharmonious and the frequency with which this has been a good thing. Conversely, it now appears that the Church is often furthest from pursuing its own best interests in those moments and places when it appears to be operating most harmoniously. For then it is all too likely that harmony will be less the result of a free and loving unanimity of

Catholics than of a fear of disharmony—the fear that since the Church is the great metaphor of harmony to be less than completely harmonious is to be less than itself.

Men cannot, of course, help dreaming of harmony because they cannot help striving for order and control. Without some measure of harmony human effort is frustrated and dialogue turns into war, cold or hot. There are worse things to pray for. Faith itself assumes the possibility of achieving such harmony as man needs. But it is a mistake to make harmony an object of conscious pursuit. Harmony, like peace of mind, is not what you seek but what you get, in some measure, if you act properly and are lucky. Neurotic persons do not need to strive for peace of mind; they need to understand what their painful symptoms are trying to tell them about themselves. In proportion as they understand the symptoms they will get, not the impossible peace of mind they dream of, but a release from the crippling and painful preoccupation with that dream.

Catholics, then, should pray less for harmony than for courage and charity. If we bear with one another charitably while courageously examining our present disharmony for its meaning we may find ourselves in the possession of such harmony as we need.

3

Sweet Dream of Liberation

Readers of Arthur Koestler's *Darkness at Noon,* especially if they are Catholics, are likely to remember the chill with which they read the epigraph to "The Second Hearing."

> When the existence of the Church is threatened, she is released from the commandments of morality. With unity as the end, the use of every means is sanctified, even cunning, treachery, violence, simony, prison, death. For all order is for the sake of the community, and the individual must be sacrificed to the common good.

This statement is ascribed to the work *De Schismate* by Dietrich von Nieheim (or Niem), Bishop of Verden. It should be made clear at once that there was such a person and such a work in which these words may be found. Dietrich, in fact, was an important functionary at the Council of Constance (1414-1418), which managed not only to burn John Hus but end the Great Western Schism. As the above quotation might lead one to suspect, he lived in desperate times: in a Europe devastated by the Black Death, wracked with Church-State tensions, exacerbated by heretic, millenarian and inquisitor, demoralized by a papacy located for a time under two heads, then under three.

But we do not really have to be told about the desperate times that provide context for Dietrich's statement. For us any such assertion of the totalitarian idea all too clearly has behind it the discovery that disunity is the prime evil. The accents of this voice are entirely familiar. It is the voice of Hitler or Stalin or Mussolini, of course, but before that it is the voice of the embattled institution giving expression to the deep-seated human fear that unless an absolute can be established there will be no rallying point against chaos.

However, Dietrich's terrible words have a different meaning in his context than in Koestler's. Dietrich belonged with the antipapalist party that was arguing the legitimacy of a council convened not by the Pope but for the purpose of electing a pope, who would then, hopefully, remain subordinate to the council. Compared with an extremist like Hus, Dietrich was even something of a moderate. Nevertheless, it is not hard to see why Koestler, concerned with the quite different problem of the person's efforts to disentangle himself from the institution, would be delighted to discover it.

Rubashov, Koestler's central figure, is indeed a most familiar modern protagonist; he is caught up in a tragic version of an action that is comic (in an older sense of the term) in Joyce's *Portrait of the Artist as a Young Man*. Both fictions belong with a great body of literature that is at once cause and effect of our conviction that the institution is the Other, The Enemy, and that authentic personal life is possibly only in proportion as the divorce from it is complete. In this dramatic conflict it is the State (ideally, the Communist State) and the Church (ideally, the Catholic Church) that most satisfactorily embody the villain, who is the champion of all those forces seen as standing against the person's impulse to enlarge himself, to love and live more fully. Of course, the villain has other manifestations: technology, the middle class, society at large, the corporation, the establishment— whatever in life operates institutionally to crib, cabin and confine the person.

The hero in this conflict must, conversely, be vigorously anarchic and antinomian as he resists institutional restriction in the interest of that intrepid consumption of experience, or pursuit of a private image, that will lead to an enlargement of personality and a more authentic life. If he is an artist or entertainer he has, to begin with, the advantage of a traditional dispensation from institutional norms. But he may also be a playboy, a hippie, a draft card burner, a motorcycle hoodlum, a homosexual, a dope-addict, an alcoholic, a sex athlete, a psychedelic adventurer. Whatever form he takes, he must be seen as a valiant rejector of the institution's demand that he sacrifice to its constricting objectives his needs as a private person.

This conflict is the dramatic expression of what might be called the sweet dream of personal liberation, the polar opposite of which is the institution's sweet dream of harmony, in which the same figures appear but with reversed values. The polarization constitutes a kind of dialectic melodrama that coarsens the whole issue, making it difficult to understand the interdependence of person and institution.

For one thing, the polarization of the two dreams makes it hard to see the extent to which institutions (which tend to conserve and bind into a unit) produce their own opposition through a failure to integrate and control their values. Thus the institution of government in America depends for its success on a considerable degree of integration of egalitarian and libertarian impulses. In the abstract it may seem clear that true personal freedom rightly understood (perhaps by God) cannot be won at the expense of one's fellow citizens or the common good. In actual fact, however, the American tradition has a strong, and no doubt energy-generating, bias for anarchy. This bias is carried along in a heady body of rhetoric and sanctified by an impressive pantheon of heroes ranging from Roger Williams to Allen Ginsberg. Historically, America can be seen as an attempt to so institutionalize itself that Americans will be discouraged from taking the sweet dream of liberation out of its controlling context. But in the meantime the cultural atmosphere is charged with excitement, for at any moment it is possible to defy the institution in the name of values it must acknowledge.

The same thing is true of the Church, which is engaged in the riskiest of enterprises: the effort to institutionalize the human drive for the greatest possible spiritual liberation. In its normal function it produces anti-institutionalists the way an emery wheel produces sparks. Historically, it has not been able to pursue its objectives without nurturing anarchists and antinomians who find it a strait jacket with respect to the realization of its own values. So saints are often hard to distinguish from heretics and paranoiac visionaries, just as in America figures like Thoreau and Whitman are often hard to distinguish from potheads and imitation beatniks. This is why Norman Cohn's *The Pursuit of the Millenium,* which is about the consequences of the sweet dream of liberation in medieval Europe, can be so instructively read not only by modern Catholics but by students of American culture.

More disastrous, however, is the extent to which the polarity of person and institution keeps us from realizing the vital interinvolvement of ourselves and institutions: the extent to which we are products of institutions and institutions are products of us. The intimacy of this involvement is pointed up by an "exchange" of views between St. Paul and T. S. Eliot. The letter kills but the spirit gives life, says St. Paul (2 Corinthians, 3-6), to which T. S. Eliot (in an essay on D. H. Lawrence) counters that the spirit kills but the letter gives life. As poetic generalizations, one statement is as true as the other; to apprehend the truth about the interdependence of spirit (in our context, meaning for persons) and letter (institutional form in which meaning is expressed) one must manage to hold both in mind. If we prefer to hold with St. Paul and let T. S. Eliot go it is not out of any great sympathy with Paul's total view of things (he is after all a great Christian institutionalist); it is rather that we find him useful in our efforts to theorize and justify our bias against institution.

(I am referring here to the familiar anti-institutional interpretation of St. Paul's words, and it is this interpretation that I conceive T. S. Eliot to be countering. What the Saint's words meant in their own context is another matter. According to C. H. Dodd in *Gospel and Law,* for instance, it is hardly likely that St. Paul meant to give comfort to Corinthian antinomians.)

St. Paul in this biased view reads like the champion of a primitive freedom that Christianity and civilization have lost—as if he were anticipating our own postclassical tendency to look to the primitive for an image of relief from the pressure of institutions. But the primitive society tends to be extremely traditional and institutional. It keeps the individual closely bound to the group, in the members of which it repeats its integrating formulas with relatively little resistance and variation. Primitive societies can be looked at as devices for keeping the self-aware individual from appearing in a context that has no place for him. They handle the problem of freedom as we understand it by keeping it from arising.

But once the primitive society has become the subject of one of those hybrid unions, that, as Marshall McLuhan puts it in *Understanding Media*, "breed furious release of energy and change," distance begins to open up between the institution and its members, and among its members, so that the self-aware person becomes possible. Acted upon and reacting to time, change and adversary, the institution becomes, however reluctantly, a liberating force, not only with respect to the person but with respect to its own meanings. For short of divine intervention, the institution that has not achieved a measure of critical direction by loosening its grip on the person remains simply the prisoner of its own history. The institution cannot imprison the person without imprisoning itself.

Actually, our sense of the person is the consequence of the energy- and distance-generating interplay of all the institutions of western civilization, especially of Church and State. Where Church and State exist together most harmoniously as a "primitive" unit the self-aware person is least likely to appear, or his efforts to free himself from the double grip of Church and State are most likely to be tragic. The American classic for this effort is the *Scarlet Letter,* in the first chapter of which the prison door and the wild rose bush symbolize the alternatives a theocracy offers as means of protecting itself: either the security of its rigid orthodoxy or abandonment to hostile elemental forces. In this polarized environment the lovers, Hester Prynne and Arthur Dimmesdale, literally have no place to go where their love will not be destructive.

But it is the very inhospitality of the Puritan society to the person that makes it a favorable environment in which to dramatize the person, if only in his death-birth pangs. This dramatization is possible only because of the advantage of a point of view in time from which, in great part because of the separation of Church and State, the conflict can be seen as having a different meaning. This is why Hawthorne's masterpiece is closer to *Darkness at Noon* than to *Lady Chatterley's Lover*, which it otherwise so closely resembles. In the modern world it is totalitarianism that exercises the double grip of theocracy, and yet it is in the iron world of totalitarianism that the person is most violently born again—provided, of course, that the free person is imaginable in that world. He is imaginable in Koestler's novel because the novel views Rubashov's plight from the vantage point of institutionally developed values that make him imaginable. Similarly, the Nazis' attempt to exterminate the Jews defines the person in the starkest terms, but this meaning is available only to an institutionally developed point of view "outside" that atrocity.

Rubashov's Russia, like Hitler's Germany, was a secular theocracy and therefore a person-strangling monopoly. "Monopolies," Pope Paul wrote in 1967 to the central committee of the Spanish Social Week, "tend to distort the truth as they tend to preserve their own interests." It is not hard to imagine the consternation with which some Spanish authorities read these words, convinced as they must have been (and apparently still are) that to allow greater political freedom is to allow greater religious freedom as well. But surely their consternation could not have been greater than that of the Italian Right with the "Marxist" overtones in the encyclical that had appeared earlier in the year. The heartening truth about "On the Development of Peoples" was that it expressed an institutionally developed point of view that was critically outside the attempt of the state to monopolize the person by uniting itself "theocratically" with a true faith—capitalism. In effect (and, in view of Church history, ironically) the Pope in this encyclical placed an official voice of the Church on the side of the separation and competition of institutions.

D. H. Lawrence's lovers, faced with the same institutional demand as Rubashov and Hawthorne's lovers, are much more fortunately situated, for in their time and place both the separation and competition of institutions have made a protective enclave for them. They have some place to go to pursue an intenser life as loving persons, and though they may be nagged at and penalized wherever they go, the institutional complexity of civilization will ultimately protect them. As a matter of fact, if they had waited a generation they would not have to go anywhere but would have been able quite openly and safely to set up housekeeping in Mellor's hut. In such circumstances, however, they would have meant much less to us, since as persons and lovers they would not have been refined and defined in contention with institutions.

Constance Chatterley and her gamekeeper might appear now as a rather staid couple motivated by a middle class desire to settle down in domestic bliss. They remain, nevertheless, legendary exem-

plars of the sweet dream of liberation from institutional constraint in its most acceptable modern
terms, which is to say sexual terms. It is not sur-
prising that the dream of liberation takes this sexual form. Sexual freedom is an important factor in
personal realization (often, of course, in heretical
or antisocial contexts), and for this reason persons
in their sexual capacity have always made Church
and State apprehensive. Thoreau in his celibate
cabin, therefore, appears (deceptively) as not
nearly the social menace that Lawrence's gamekeeper is. What is against Lawrence is a conventional wisdom about sex that wants to keep it
below the belt: that prefers the supervised bawdy
house, both as a safety valve for man's "baser"
instincts and as a protection from pressure to consider these instincts in a larger and more trouble-
some context. This is because in life as in art sexual
freedom tends to be symbolic freedom. By the
same token, people who still adhere to institutional
standards tend to see a widespread rejection of
traditional sexual norms as symbolic of a general
loss of control. Our fantasies of an anxiety-free
utopia and of universal disaster are both orgasmic.

But whether sexual or not. the sweet dream of
liberation assumes the possibility of a deinstitutionalized life. In actual fact, however, the apparently deinstitutionalized man remains linked to
and determined by institutions in subtle ways—
not the least important of which is his dependence

on an institutionally protected enclave in which he can assert and enjoy some measure of real or apparent disengagement. But if he is not vitally linked to institutions he will (like Hester Prynne) suffer from alienation and anomie. These agonies he may accept stoically, even heroically, as simply the price of freedom. The more likely thing, however, is that he will avoid some of the pains of deinstitutionalization by becoming an institution sampler. The effect of the enclave created for the person by the competition and interaction of modern institutions is that of a supermarket in which values abstracted from the structures and disciplines in which they were nurtured appear abundantly available. Institution-samplers (or seekers, as they may more honorifically be called) can be important gadflies or sources of enrichment to established institutions. But cut off from the vital life of institutions they tend also to repeat the earlier mistakes of institutions, and so get themselves into the kinds of trouble that make them interesting to novelists and playwrights.

The more practical way to avoid the agonies of alienation and anomie that attend deinstitutionalization is to reinstitutionalize the experience of and means to a particular form of liberation. Thus Dr. Timothy Leary attempted a few years ago to gather up the loose ends of LSD liberation into a rather campish kind of gnosticism which he proposed as a new religion. The weakness of psychedelic liberation as a continuing force in the life of the individual and society is its lack of structure and definition—the very qualities that make it appealing. Unless, therefore, it is contained within established scientific, social or religious structures it tends to be simply a rapsodic and random form of deinstitutionalization. Dr. Leary apparently wanted to make it more than that; his religion even had clear links with traditional Christianity, upon which it leaned for support much as Voodoo does.

Whatever may be the controlled and institutionalized future of such liberating agencies as the psychedelic drugs, it is apparent that to many people they seem to prove the possibility of an effortless expansion of personality, and by the same token to prove the radical and inimical otherness of the institution. If the institution is in some sense responsible for the liberation of the person, the implied reasoning seems to be, then its proper evolutionary destiny is, like that of the Marxist state, to wither away—as it has indeed withered away in those erotic Polynesian fantasies with which Hollywood once responded to the institutional pressures of modern civilization. That the pressures are defining and limiting factors in the utopian response, that they are the discipline in which it is grounded, is not so apparent.

Neither is it so apparent to the impatient Christian today that the dream of personal liberation, in which spirit can be cherished apart from contaminating letter, is determined by the institutional Church and grounded in its discipline. The traditional language with which we try to understand the relation of letter and spirit predisposes us to imagine discipline and structure as that against which spirit naturally and properly chafes, rather than that through which spirit is discovered and its potencies realized. We tend to assume a disjunction of letter and spirit that recalls an older disjunction of body and soul—one that supported an ascetic denial of what we now call the person in the interest of spiritual liberation. At its most extreme, as in the Desert Fathers, this disjunction inspired a dream of liberation that similarly stretched the bond between person and institution to the breaking point. When St. Paul (called the first hermit) meets St. Anthony in the Syrian Desert it is as if the last two men on earth have come together. "Tell me, I pray thee," says Paul, "how fares the human race: if new roofs be risen in the ancient cities, whose empire it is that now sways the world; and if any still survive, snared in the error of the demons." And the haunting words almost imply the irrelevancy of the institutionalized Church as means to man's liberation and salvation.

The Desert Fathers too cultivated the psychedelic mode in their fashion: they aspired to an expanded consciousness. "By the very exaggeration of their lives," says Helen Waddell, they "stamped infinity on the imagination of the West." The heritage is an ambiguous one, for it is the imagination stamped with infinity that most passionately dreams of liberation and is most exacerbated by the strictures of institution. It is this imagination that explains so much in those "strange alternations of rigorism and antinomianism" that enliven not only the story of the Desert Fathers but the whole history of the Church. What Miss Waddell helps us see, really, is the extent to which the Fathers' athletic denial of the person and the letter of the world in the interest of liberating the spirit prepared the way for those who would subsequently deny the letter of the Church in the interest of liberating person and spirit. The Fathers, tantalized by the vision of a "haven of invulnerable living," risked, says Miss Waddell, "a kind of treason to the *civitas Dei.*"

It is a treason the sweet dream of liberation always tempts one to, driven as it is by a pastoral yearning for clarity and simplicity. The person-institution relationship, especially in the Church, is far too complex and mysterious to be tolerable to one possessed by this yearning. Institutions, whether sacred or secular, are the structures in which men define themselves in their various relationships and capacities, and in which they both conserve and learn the full import of their values. It is within the institution, especially as it is pressed by time, change and adversary, that the person becomes critically aware of himself and the institution as in some sense separate and yet inseparable. The mystery in this relationship results not so much from the fact that it is unknowable as from the fact of "a surplusage of meaning in the known," as Nathan B. Scott, Jr., puts it in another connection.

This surplusage of meaning in the known is what accounts for the lag of theory behind the experienced fact of institutional life—a lag that is at least as great as the lag of the institutional Church behind the full potential of its deposit of faith. We know in part and we theorize in part, and if there is not a protective element of irony in our theorizing we are imprisoned in our theories as securely as we ever were in our institutions. Our nonironic theories, in fact, tend to become extremely constricting counter-institutions. So the theory of a deinstitutionalized Church, in which the spirit of Christianity is liberated from the corrupting letter, points only to an anomic state out of which new versions of familiar tyrannies arise.

There is no better or more instructive place to see this paradox at work than in the world of Dietrich of Nieheim. The theory of the relationship between individual and Church implied in Dietrich's statement anticipates Doestoevsky's Grand Inquisitor and is of course heretical. It assumes, in fact, an institutional antinomianism, the counterpart of which is to be found in the contemporary Free Spirit movement, a medieval heresy which provides some colorful moments in Ronald Knox's *Enthusiasm* and to which Norman Cohn devotes two fascinating chapters in his *Pursuit of the Millenium.*

The heresy of the Free Spirit presents all the familiar characteristics: a rejection of all institutional authority, particularly that of Church and State; a system of self-exaltation and a pursuit of total emancipation; a quasi-mystical evaluation of the sexual act; a conviction of nonrational access to, or pantheistic identification with, ultimate sources of power and meaning; a recapturing of primitive blessedness and innocence in which traditional moral distinctions are irrelevant; the protective and ritual resort to an arcane language; the sense of godhead achieved if not transcended.

The imagination of infinity (that powerful deterrent to irony) has never been more flamboyantly at work in Western civilization. The Brethern of the Free Spirit act out the sweet dream of liberation for us in the clarifying dimensions of caricature. Having rejected the strictures of institution, they violently institutionalized their freedom. They make it plain that outside institution one is most likely to find not freedom but only the liberated diseases of institution.

4

The Escalation Bends

We live in an escalating world and most of us suffer to one degree or another from the escalation bends, the spiritual equivalent of those excruciating pains the diver experiences when he ascends too rapidly from a level at which he was comfortable to one in which he is not yet prepared to live. We suffer the bends simultaneously in so many contexts—economic, social, political, theological— that we have difficulty determining the exact source of our pain. Would the encyclical "Of Human Life" bother us so much if its central issue, the definition of authority in an accelerating environment, were not at the same time wracking the communist world and the world of American politics?

45

The familiar form of the escalation bends—identity crisis, anomie, sense of betrayal, crisis of faith, disgust with the corruptions of civilized society, sense of impending doom—all relate to the problem of authority and therefore to the problem of person and institution. If we could relate ourselves to institutions as intimately as we once did (and as numerous voices tell us we still ought to) we would not suffer the bends, or at least the pains would be greatly reduced, for one of the functions of an institution is to moderate the rate of escalation—even on occasion to serve as a decompression chamber. But the pains would at least be easier to bear if we knew how to talk about the relation between person and institution. We have trouble talking about this relationship because so much of our attention has been concentrated on the need to keep suspiciously apart from institutions.

Institutions are the communal and social aspects of ourselves; they are the Other, the Enemy, only insofar as we are alienated from a part of ourselves. If we cannot talk about them properly it is because we cannot talk about ourselves properly. The fact that we have been conditioned to think disjunctively of the relation between person and institution keeps us from understanding our dependence as persons on the dialectical engagement between two aspects of ourselves—one aspect that structures and conserves achieved or revealed values, another that examines these in the light of the fresh information and unexpected perspectives that press upon institutionalized persons. This is why J. M. Cameron speaks of "that senseless opposition between man as social and man as individual." "There can be no substitute for institutions," says the sociologist Nathan Glazer, "even though they may become tired, bureaucratic, and corrupt." There can be no substitute for them because there is no substitute for persons.

One of the historical functions of the institution, especially as it interrelates and competes with other institutions, is to create critical distance between itself and the individual. If it could not do this the person as we know him could not be born, nor could the institution be kept relevant to the needs of persons. But it cannot give birth to the person without revealing its corruptions to him and running the risk of his disillusionment. Hence that close link between personal freedom and disaffection with institutions that is one of the hallmarks of the modern world. We have made the exhilarating discovery that our institutions are sitting ducks for the discovery of corruption that promises liberation. Practically anything one can say against the major institutions of civilization is true in some perspective or other, and most perspectives are self-validating: angled at their objects in such a way as to produce effortlessly and endlessly the evidence that substantiates their initial assumptions. So our culture is hounded by those visions of deinstitutionalized liberation that are unwittingly caricatured in cosmetic ads and in the polymorphous perversities of the psychedelic Left.

It is not hard to see how painfully Christians, especially Catholics, can be caught between authorities in such a time: between authority as traditionally structured in the Church and the authority of the person whose freedom and integrity seem eternally threatened by institutions, between conscience as conformity to institutional mandates and conscience as the expression of personal autonomy. They are torn between the image of the Church as Mother and the image of it as Other and so repeat the ancient ambivalence toward the womb: Is it a source of life to be cherished or a prison to be escaped from?

This is particularly true of Catholics who have over-identified with the Church in its juridical aspect. In all institutions there is a force at work that encourages such an over-identification simply in the interests of order and security, and so encourages the formula "to obey is to believe." As a result, every error, vagary or corruption in the juridical process produces a crisis of faith (as was once the case with those Marxists who had over-identified with Russian communism). This is why the concept of a loyal opposition within the Church is as scandalous to disaffected as to ultramontane Catholics. For both it is a matter of either/or. In a time of crisis institutions in their housekeeping functions (whether headquartered in Rome, Moscow or Washington) tend to paint themselves into corners by reducing the options in this fashion. The reduction can appear as an authentic and agonizing dilemma that proposes either total and unquestioning obedience or defection. One function of a loyal opposition is to show that this is a pseudo-dilemma.

The formula "to obey is to believe" with its dangerous over-emphasis on the juridical Church is also the formula for a false security. In effect it tends to remove the burden of faith by shifting it to the institution. Now Catholics are discovering what Protestants have long known: that their fair share of this burden can be an appalling load. At heart many Catholics, even liberal Catholics, yearn for an ecclesiastical Eisenhower to usher in a new age of normalcy in which the Church will reassume their burdens in old-style triumphal fashion but in terms they can accept. The aggiornamento was supposed to be an invigorating opening of windows, the triumphant emergence (as many of us saw it) of the Church Triumphant into the modern world: ecumenism, overtures to the communists, a swinging theology, the vernacular mass with the turned-around altar, the updated nun, the emergent layman, the primacy of conscience, the new honesty about the old corruptions, no more index, no more fish on Friday. In the euphoria of innovation few bargained for the searching and agonizing reappraisals that, we are beginning to see, renewal really means—and which, no doubt, those who opposed the Council to begin with sensed long before anyone else.

In the meantime, many who initially were exhilarated now feel disillusioned, disoriented and deceived, having discovered that renewal is not terminal and that the new freedom entails unanticipated burdens and anxieties. So the current Catholic hyper-sensitivity to the corruptions in the Church, which in one context is a sign of vitality and genuine concern, in another context is simply the expression of a need to be revenged against a betrayer and to punish oneself for having allowed oneself to be betrayed.

To many Catholics who are tormented by the escalation bends the distinction between a structured and unstructured Church is therefore understandably attractive, since it holds out the promise of separating the pure essence of Christ's message from the dross of the organized Church. This is a reversal of Christ's message not to separate the weeds from the wheat until the harvest lest the wheat be harmed in the process, but it is in accord with a modern apocalyptic spirit that is compelled by the impatient dream of pure deinstitutionalized liberation. This pure Church would of course be nonhierarchic, for hierarchy is seen as cause and protector of corruption.

Such a vision (and who is not compelled by it to some degree?) is more symptomatic than prophetic. Even in the world of Eros Triumphant, Herbert Marcuse concedes, there will be hierarchy. Hierarchy, however designated, is the means men use to protect their freedom to pursue certain values. In times of rapid change the danger is not merely that it will be too rigid to reappraise itself but that it will not not stand firm against backlash impulses generated by the fear of disorder. Backlash, as Governor Wallace is helping us to see, is the expression of loss of nerve, and hierarchy should be seen as the preparations made in advance against it—preparations based on the realization that when backlash is a real possibility there is always at least as much danger of losing what clarity and freedom have been won as of not gaining more.

When hierarchy does not hold fast to what has been achieved and clarified there is no standing ground from which to go further, no clear position to engage with and against which to test new formulations. In practical terms this means that in sharply escalating times it may be at least as important for the hierarchy of the Church to close ranks against disgruntled or panicky reactionaries as to open its arms to the avantgarde. Even when hierarchy itself is divided, as it is now on the issue of birth control, it is important for the divisions to emphasize common ground lest a vacuum be created into which the familiar tyrannies, promising the familiar freedoms, rush triumphantly.

We inherit from the Enlightenment a tendency to believe that no such vacuum can result, that corruption comes from institutions so that any harm to them is clear gain. At the same time, the modern communication media intensify our innate corruption-consciousness. Corrupt events make the most satisfactory information, but this information in turn has a capacity to make corrupt events. Information about corruption is itself one of the most satisfactory and addictive of events. Corruption is where the action is. We need to know it in all its dimensions, locations and causes and in its most sensational contexts, but this need is complicated by the need to locate it outside ourselves in a way that alleviates the burden of guilt and anxiety that is a consequence of our relative freedom within institutional structures. To discover that the world is sufficiently corrupt (as it always is if one can find a way of looking at it closely enough) can be a moral relief. To discover that the Church which has burdened one with commitments and moral injunctions is corrupt can be a downright joy: we can be released from it, perhaps even transported beyond good and evil.

The mass of Catholic corruption literature that has appeared since Vatican II belongs in the category of exposé and has the range one would expect to find in any sizable body of exposé writing: at its best it is a necessary function of renewal; at its middle best it is a therapeutic release of tension; at its worst it is sensational exploitation. Catholic exposé, like secular exposé, shades off into a pornography of violence in which the Church simply becomes a monster metaphor of corruption: that Whore of Babylon that held the world of the Reformation in such lurid fascination.

The parallel with the pornography of violence in secular exposé is instructive. In the latter the prime subject is the false promise of sex as objectified in a woman who apparently offers infinite bliss in a sensual utopia, but who after having been proven utterly corrupt is killed with satisfactory violence. This story serves a complexity of needs, the majority of which are symptomatic of corruptions in the reader. Most important among them are the need to be revenged on a betrayer and the need to degrade in order to exorcize. Always in the background is a need to establish, at least in a negative way, one's own purity, and a genuine fear that one will lose control in the presence of irresistible attraction. None of these needs can be satisfied apart from a fiction in which the victim is doomed to corruption by being held to impossible standards.

All of this is present in the pornography of Catholic exposé: revenge on the betrayer Church; degradation in order to exorcize (if the Church can be made to appear bad enough we may be able to resist its attractions); negative establishment of one's own purity (the more corrupt the Church can be made to appear the less corrupt we are); control of the degrading process by holding the institutional Church to impossible pre-Vatican II standards. In the secular pornography of violence the ultimate and perverse rationale is the need to abstract the woman in order to reject her as a person. In the Catholic pornography of corruption the terrifying need one often senses working below the surface is the need to abstract the Church in order to reject Christ. Once it was possible to protect oneself from Christ by making an idol of the Church; now one can achieve the same end by making the Church into a negative idol.

The fierce dialectic between idol and negative idol torments those trying to stay in the Church as well as those who having gotten out are trying to stay out. It is a dialectic of misplaced love and of the misplaced hate that it generates. Perhaps one is never really in the Church till he can stop loving it for the wrong reasons, and never really out of it till he can stop hating it for the wrong reasons.

The most powerful instance in our literature of a man caught in the dialectic of idol and negative idol is Shakespeare's Othello. The intensity with which he sees Desdemona as his negative idol (a whore) is in relation to the intensity with which he previously saw her as a goddess. The lost idol is always in his mind to torment him. One might be tempted to say that he must kill the negative idol in order to find the real woman behind the idol: that the killing is a supreme and heroic act of discovery. Certainly the play has this meaning for iconoclasts: handle idols and negative idols gently for there may be live bodies behind them. It is at least as likely, however, that Othello discovers only that he has killed Desdemona the idol in order to preserve the idol he has placed against her, and that only the play knows the real woman.

Othello's counter-idol is his honor ("For naught I did in hate, but all in honor," he says after the murder). He is like the rest of us: to be meaningfully alive he must sense himself to be located near the pure. When the pure Desdemona is proven to him to be corrupt she is sacrificed to the only purity he has left—and against which she has been defined. And the terrible implication is that she was always valuable to him primarily as a means to the end of his honor. But this is the way it is with our idolatries: they confuse our need to serve, to commit ourselves, with our need to be served, to be the subjects of commitment.

Othello is a relatively primitive figure trapped in a legendary view of himself and reality, yet nothing in Shakespeare is more meaningful to us than his tragic impatience for purity and the tragic egotism of his effort to find a constant of purity and security within himself. Our temptation when our institutions appear to fail us in their corruption is

similarly to idolize our honor in currently acceptable terms: honesty, integrity, self-respect. The
temptation is correlative with our inclination to
understand the institution as a threatening Other,
to be tolerated only insofar as it serves our integrity. The result for many disaffected Catholics now
is a genuinely tragic dilemma since they retain
some sense of the loneliness and sterility of such a
stand, some sense that one's own integrity cannot
be itself a prime reason for action but only the consequence of a self-transcending commitment.

The escalation bends, whether Othello's or our
own, always express themselves as an impatience
with impurity that is also a radical impatience with
time and a failure to understand that to speed up
time is to speed up its iconoclastic function. Exis-
tentially speaking, the rate of the flow of time depends on the rate of the flow of information. It is
the knowledge explosion made possible by the pro-
liferation and interaction of media that makes it
possible to question the ideal structures that were
once the sources of our comfort and security by
showing them in new perspectives and relationships. We cannot say that our institutions are ab-
solutely speaking more corrupt than they once
were; we know only that more of their corruption
has been revealed to us and that information about
corruption is itself an escalating thing.

In a situation of rising expectations corruption
tends to become intolerable in proportion as the

time rate increases. So we have that modern impatient straining against time which is really a desire
that time run quickly to an ideal stopping point
beyond corruption. This is true for the person as
well as for the institution: accelerating time brings
him a potentially demoralizing flood of information
about his own corruption. This is why he has never
needed Church and State in their scapegoat functions as he needs them now. Conversely, as Father
Charles Curran points out in his contribution to
the "Jesus" issue of *Commonweal*, "One who real-
izes the difficulty in breaking away from his own
selfishness and sinfulness also understands the
slowness of growth in the structures of human existence."

The escalation bends are simply the "feel" of
modern life, but the Catholic tends to feel them
with a special intensity because of the protected
condition in which he arrives in the modern world.
He is crisis-of-faith-prone because of the extent to
which he has shifted the burden of faith to the institutional Church. Having for so long used the
comforts of religion to escape from the experience
of religion, he is in a particularly good position to
be demoralized by the normal growing pains of the
human spirit, and perhaps more easily dismayed
than other Christians to discover the radically fidu-
ciary nature of human experience, even in its most
objective and scientific dimensions.

"We must now recognize belief once more as

the source of all knowledge," the scientist-human-ist Michael Polanyi states in his powerful book *Personal Knowledge.* This view of human experience—in which, ironically, Augustine is found to be in important respects more relevant to modern science than Locke—throws special emphasis on the connection between personal development and the crisis of faith, and on the mistake of attempting to organize human life in such terms of purity and certainty as to make crises of faith impossible. The traditional fear of the crisis of faith is part of the pathology of Christianity. We need to see it for what it is: not only as the apprehension of irrecoverable loss but as the fear of a conversion that will destroy the comforts of a spiritual status quo. "Men," says Gregory Baum, "are transformed by God through many conversions." But faced with this arduous program men also prefer the luxury of the pure and the secure.

Such a preference cannot be separated from the nervousness and excitability that Catholics—especially American Catholics—display when the Church is caught up in controversial situations. The human condition is one in which more or less opposed perspectives move in their contention towards consensus and are opposed by fresh perspectives as they approach it. Pure consensus is a dream that implies the end of time and the end of process, but it is a dream that cripples those many Catholics, liberal and conservative, to whom the fundamentally dialectic nature of human knowing is offensive, if not downright frightening. Such Catholics—and the fault is by no means entirely theirs—make dilemmas for themselves and others as naturally as birds make nests. They are, I suspect, the ones Karl Rahner has in mind when, in his brilliant statement on the recent encyclical, he observes that the Magisterium cannot be placed "in each case in this dilemma—either to speak with its highest and infallible authority or keep silent."

It is the passion for purity and security that also leads so many of us to use conditional commitment as a technique of survival. Conditional commitment, being impatient, operates by threat and ultimatum. In substance it defines the Church in limited terms and then says to it: I will commit myself *provided*. It keeps the option of defection open both as a lever against the Church and as a protection against the consequences of over-commitment. Assuming the radical otherness of the institution, it both anticipates and courts betrayal.

The opposite of conditional commitment is charitable commitment. Charity is the Christian's technique for survival, though if it is valued simply as technique it is nothing. Charity is a way of enduring with partial knowledge in the face of the apparently irreconcilable, the contradictory, the absurd, and is thus in certain respects like those other techniques of survival that rely upon irony or a sense of the complementary nature of reality.

Like them it is a protection against the impatience for purity and certainty that does so much to create the conditions that torment us.

However, the recognition of the ironic and complementary nature of the human condition may result in little more than a holding action, and may ultimately serve as justification for that conditional commitment which we have learned to identify with our integrity. But the commitment of charity, that "yet more excellent way," as St. Paul designates it to the Corinthians, is not put off by partial knowledge or by the puzzling reflections in the mirror. There is nothing it cannot face; "there is no limit to its faith, its hope, and its endurance." For the Catholic this charitable commitment may not be a way out of the escalation bends; it may not even mitigate them very much; it is simply the only meaningful way he has of living with them as he shoulders the burden of his personhood in this kind of world.

5

The Tyranny of Virtue

In 1682 a distinguished American wrote as follows to his fellow New England clergyman, "Ye aged and Beloved, Mr. John Higginson":

There be now at sea a ship called Welcome, which has on board 100 or more of the heretics and malignants called Quakers, with W. Penn, who is the chief scamp, at the head of them. The General Court has accordingly given sacred orders to Master Malachi Huscott, of the brig Porpoise, to waylay the said Welcome slyly as near the Cape of Cod as may be, and make captive the said Penn and his ungodly crew, so that the Lord may be glorified and not mocked on the soil of this new country with the heathen worship of these people. Much spoil can be made of selling the whole lot to Barbadoes, where slaves fetch good prices in rum and sugar, and we shall not only do the Lord great good by punishing the wicked, but we shall make great good for his ministers and people.

> Yours in the bowels of Christ,
>   —Cotton Mather

The situation has a grim sportiveness about it (welcome, indeed!), but it is not easy to believe that it had that value for Cotton Mather: he lacked the ability of Shakespeare's Henry V to see the continuity between the practical joke and the strategy of great affairs. Nor is it likely that he was conscious of a cynical exploitation of religion for profit. Most probably he quite sincerely believed that it was God's will that the righteous inherit the earth in the interest of His glorification. Cotton's theocratic worldview, founded as it was on a sense of crisis, was crisis-prone, so that extreme measures in defense of virtue were both mandatory and automatic. He was a "good" Machiavellian who knew the enemy when he saw him: that chief scamp, William Penn, was after all a notorious advocate of religious tolerance and as such threatened to reduce that vital pressure which in Cotton's world was a condition to the perception of meaning and value.

Historically, the accents of Cotton Mather's letter are familiar enough. We hear them earlier in the century in the English Puritan Parliament's order "that no person shall be employed but such as the House shall be satisfied of his real godliness"; or in Dietrich von Nieheim's assertion, early in the fifteenth century, that "when the existence of the Church is threatened, she is released from the commandments of morality" in the interests of unity and the common good; or now in Herbert Marcuse's assertion (in *An Essay on Liberation*) that since in a democracy majorities may choose wrongly in terms of their best interests, therefore necessary social change cannot take place "through the rules and methods of democratic legality." Always the spirit behind the words is the spirit behind Savonarola's great bonfire on the Piazza della Signoria in Florence, a hecatomb that consumed cosmetics, jewelry, musical instruments, chessboards, playing cards, books, precious manuscripts and paintings of famous beauties: and meanwhile, according to Jacob Burckhardt, "the air echoed with song, the sound of trumpets, and the pealing of bells."

This is the paradoxical tyranny of virtue: paradoxical because its promise and hope is liberation, not bondage. It is also the human predicament: our tyrannies begin in our virtues, yet without a firm commitment to virtue not only is it impossible to sense ourselves as meaningfully alive but it is quite possible that evil will overwhelm us. For this reason it is necessary in our own permissive times to express sensual extravagance, even the production and sale of pornography, in a context of moral crusade—so that, as has often been observed, the more uninhibited young (and not so young) are able to act like libertines while talking like puritans, thereby repeating the combination of erotic license and religiosity that marked many medieval heretical movements.

The trouble, of course, is not with virtue but with virtuous men. The human need of virtue has the urgency of an instinct, which means that entrancement by virtue is one of man's occupational hazards. The effect of entrancement is that of specialism: an intense limitation of context, a restriction of point of view, that is not recognized as such. The naivete of the entranced virtuous man is the naivete of melodrama: from the anticipated total triumph of virtue he expects only good things to result, as Cotton Mather expected only good things to result from "selling the whole lot to Barbadoes," and as Marcuse expects only good things to result from the use of "apparently undemocratic means" to silence those who oppose objective reason and virtue. As Catholics were in the habit of saying in their ghetto days (believing in their beleaguered innocence that they were the first to say it): error has no rights.

George Woodcock, the former British anarchist, has written of the part George Orwell played in his own discovery of the paradoxical tyranny of virtue. Orwell, he says, "pointed out the danger that anarchist intolerance might create a moral dictatorship which would imperil the very freedom for which anarchists claimed to fight." Woodcock himself had already discovered that "the more ded-

icated a militant, the more priggish and intolerant
he was likely to be"—a remark that might often be
applied to both liberal and conservative voices in
the post-Vatican II Church.

Dedication need not be, nor has it always been,
priggish and intolerant. Unfortunately, however,
the cause-and-effect connection is so widely accepted in our culture that we are inclined to suspect the integrity of a dedication that is neither
priggish nor intolerant (of course we substitute
more honorific terms). By the same token, prig-
gishness and intolerance are available as means if
the dedicated militant needs to assure himself of
his own dedication. This is why dedicated militants are so easily caught in escalation traps in
which substantive demands, by dissolving one
after another into symbolic demands, turn out to
be unrealizable: the state of militant dedication,
to which some people are as pathologically addicted as others are to alcohol, needs more and
more militancy to keep it alive. It is especially easy
to keep alive when religious issues are at stake—
hence the religious atmosphere in which most crusades exist.

Even when tyrannous virtue attacks what it
conceives to be corruption in the Church its style
and process are traditional: they are largely determined, that is, by saintly models, so that at the
present time the institutional Church is in the position of being embarrassed by tactics and attitudes

it must in other contexts extol. Among the community of saints there are styles for all seasons, as one might expect given the cultural and ethnic variety of Christian history. Nevertheless, the Church has for so long and in so many places been the Church Militant that it has tended to emphasize (if not on occasion create) the militancy of its saints. Christians may be aware in a corner of their minds of a tradition of grave merriness in their hagiography; nevertheless the typical saint figures to them as a nonnegotiating extremist dwelling in a black and white world whose whole life is a pattern of hyperbolic gestures, as if he were a protagonist in God's own melodrama. He dwells on a pillar, he dares to rebuke sinful kings to their faces, he licks the sores of beggars, he throws himself on thorns, he lives on crusts and water in a desert cave, he flogs himself and sleeps in a hair shirt on a bare floor, he courts a frightful martyrdom. One is tempted to say that in modern terms he tears up draft cards, harasses college administrators and the representatives of Dow Chemical, scatters blood on or destroys government records, disrupts religious services with holy wrath, hurls the terrible ultimatums of virtue against judge, president and pope.

The Saint Militant needs to be compared with the Hero Militant, for in our culture both compellingly demonstrate one way to solve problems in crisis situations. The Hero Militant, whether in literature or legend, tends also to be defined by the nonnegotiable positions he dramatically embodies. No one has more powerfully presented the complex relationships between this old-style intransigent hero and the exigencies of the civil community than Shakespeare. Such heroic prisoners of honor as Coriolanus, Othello and Hotspur are represented as figures who are tyrants of virtue because virtue has tyrannized over them. Their single-minded commitments compel admiration, their fates sympathy and awe, for in their very extremities they extend human capacities, in whatever dangerously limited contexts.

We are tempted to say that the plays accept the heroic virtues at face value but question the contexts in which they are displayed. Actually, the plays suggest that such a distinction misses the point, for the heroic contexts corrupt the virtues. When Coriolanus is confronted with the nonnegotiable demands of the tribunes (who represent the people) he nonnegotiably advises the senators to "at once pluck out the multitudinous tongue—" that is, utterly and forcibly reject these demands, some of which are just. To him, honor and accommodation or negotiation are contraries; honor (which is perfect or it is nothing) is the absolute to which mere people must always give way. The play rejects this typical heroic problem-solving as anachronistic and destructive: for to insist as Coriolanus does that the city exists to serve the needs of virtue (his virtue) is to insist that it exist in a state of tyranny. Against this passionately restrictive aspiration the play sets the vision of a polity that exists as a rational and humane order in which virtue can be pursued with a measure of real freedom. It therefore counters that tendency in our culture (powerfully spelled out by Lewis Mumford in the Spring, 1965, *Daedelus*) to use the concept of utopia as vehicle for the totalitarian impulses that have plagued our secular and sacred institutions.

Both hero and saint militant tend to create the kind of problems for which they have solutions, hence they are in important ways conservative forces: they tend, that is, to develop and react to crisis situations in ways that bind them to the saintly and heroic past. They are powerful precedents for those who, because their defining habitat is crisis, are inclined to proceed not "by process," as the Senator Menenius urges the polarized parities in *Coriolanus* to proceed, but by ad hoc departures from process—that is from the codified and legalized courses of action upon which Rome was founded. Cotton Mather and Dietrich of Nieheim unhesitatingly adopted an ad hoc morality, the implications of which were subversive to their own values. Each would have denounced a relativist position as heretical, yet each was quite capable of acting as a "momentary" relativist, as if he was dispensed because of an emergency situation from the prescriptions of traditional Christian morality. Each was apparently quite confident that he would be understood in his own world as a special case, no more a threat to virtue or orthodoxy than poetic license is to meaning.

Indeed, the "modern" element in Cotton and Dietrich is exactly this combination of absolutism and relativism—a combination that characterizes many heroes of what we know as The New Left or The Movement, counterparts of which exist in the Church. The attractiveness of this combination has to be seen as an exhilarating relief from the dead end of that moral relativism that is one aspect of traditional liberalism ("one aspect" because, after all, liberalism had its own constricting absolutes). The moral absolutism of Herbert Marcuse no less than that of the John Birch Society is a form of reactionary backlash against what is seen as a dangerous establishment relativism. Marcuse's attack on linguistic philosophy in *One Dimensional Man* is a counterpart to the Birchite attack on sensitivity training and sex education in the schools. But absolutes by themselves are too restricting for militant operations, especially against other absolutes, unless they become the sanctions (Cotton Mather's "sacred orders") for exceptional or relativist procedures of the sort usually associated with those who have no other principle than expediency.

Cotton and Dietrich also demonstrate that embattled institutions are as prone to adopt ad hoc tactics as the passionate reformers or antagonists who threaten them. Indeed (as Xavier Rynne's reports of Vatican II clearly indicated), the institution's real or suspected violations of its own announced standards become justifications for the ad hoc violations of dissenters and reformers. Hugger-mugger in pentagon, state house or curia is answered by violent confrontation or righteous law-breaking from crusading militants. This is why wise administrators, especially now, are careful not only to proceed scrupulously by process but to dispense power among the administered, for an imbalance of power becomes itself a sanction for ad hoc procedures.

But ad hoc morality, like situation ethics, is sanctioned too by the lack of "fit" between moral laws and particular cases. Men are constantly getting into (or creating) crisis situations which seem to be so unique as to be outside established procedures or norms. For crisis-prone and solipsistic personalities this is virtually all situations; since they exist in great number and attract a good deal of attention to themselves, they are often hard to distinguish from those men of good will and genuine moral imagination whose predicament, caught as they are between intolerable evil and intolerable means against it, is truly tragic—as one suspects was the case, for instance with Dietrich Bonhoeffer once he committed himself to the plot against Hitler. The idolizer of conventional morality as well as the passionate moral utopian who opposes him have prescriptions for ending this predicament, each promising "wholeness" and ease of conscience at the expense of one of the conditions of personhood.

For there is good reason to believe that Bonhoeffer's predicament is ineradicable from the human condition, that in fact it constitutes an enduring story-situation of divided loyalties in which is worked out the theme of man's discovery of himself. A modern tragic hero caught in this situation with the accumulated lessons of the past spread out in front of him must act in the anticipation of two possible consequences: extreme backlash of the powers attacked or the repressive and violent institutionalization of his own ad hoc action so that one tyranny is replaced by another. He must also consider with some dismay the company he must keep in the category in which his action will probably place him: terrorists and assassins may do badly on sanity tests but they automatically get high marks for dedication.

The paradoxical movement of militant action from liberation to tyranny (which, since alternate futures have been prevented can always be called clear gain) is facillitated by the means used to protect that limitation of perspective so necessary to militant virtue. Militant virtue needs moral absolutism, and moral absolutism expresses itself in the protective conviction that the good man will not look too closely at the good cause: that he is indeed dispensed from scrutinizing his own cause

with the intellectual severity he directs at his opposition. This is the counterpart on the rhetorical
level to the more extreme ad hoc tactics on other
levels: kidnappings, coercion by threat or blackmail, physical constraint, disruption of religious
services, harrassment of speakers, violent occupa-
tion of buildings, destruction of records, etc., all of
which are sanctioned by a polarization of virtue
and corruption that characterizes soap opera or
primitive epic.

It is this spirit of the velvet glove for the good
cause that leads the sympathetic Left, for instance,
to react to the rhetoric of the Manifesto of the
Black National Economic Conference with a leniency it refuses its opponents: indeed, with a leniency it once saw as subversive to intellectual
integrity. Leslie Fiedler's essay "Afterthoughts on
the Rosenbergs" (included in *An End to Innocence*)
is still a classic dissection of this kind of leniency.
With its emphasis on the desperate subterfuges of
symbolic truth-telling and on the natural hostility
of political and sociologic dogmatism to persons
and the truth, it is as relevant now as when it was
first published thirteen years ago—in a period
when, no less than now, ideology was corrupting
the moral imagination.

One suspects too that this leniency, now as in
the McCarthy Fifties, is often the consequence of
that moral blackmail which has always been one of
the most powerful weapons available to the dedi-

cated militant, whether he operates within or against institutions. In the most extreme terms this is his threat to burden with total guilt all those who refuse to commit themselves totally to his view and his course of action, and conversely his promise totally to absolve dedicated followers. No doubt the jubilation that attended Savonarola's bonfire had several causes, but surely that jubilation was also expressive of the exhilaration that follows on relief from an intolerable burden of guilt. The implication is not that similar ritual acts of destruction in our own time can be reduced simply to the need of a scapegoat; the implication is rather that the refusal by the sympathetic Left to recognize this need as a factor at all unless it can be used to discredit an opponent is a clear indication that ideology and intellectual treason are still the bedfellows Julien Benda said they were a half century ago.

The tyranny of the ad hoc is also made easier by our naivete about the relation between means and ends. It is a commonplace when criticizing the actions of passionate militants to distinguish their admirable causes from their violent or extra-legal means. But given the extent to which in Western civilization saint and hero have sanctified militant conduct, this is a dangerous concession: the likely thing is that the militant is already sufficiently the prisoner of his cause not to question the means that serve it. The concession is also naive because it overlooks the interdependence of ends and means. Means have a way of determining their own ends in combination with the backlash they inspire and in counteraction to which they escalate. The immoderate and ad hoc procedures of the American Temperance Movement turned it early in its history into an intemperance movement; the means used in an effort to achieve harmony in the Post Reformation Church were instrumental to the disharmony from which the Church now suffers. In both instances, self-deception, conditioned by the pressure of adversaries, disguised for a long time the fact that a significant change of ends was taking place.

It is quite true that the rejection of means often masks a disapproval of ends against which it is no longer possible to take a public stand. There are several familiar signs of this tactic: an unwillingness to allow dissidents the full range of legally or constitutionally sanctioned options; a tendency to measure dissidents by harsher standards than those who oppose them—to find tolerable in them, for instance, a reliance upon hyperbole and symbolic gesture that elsewhere in our culture is felt to be acceptable and normal; a demand for disproportionate penalties for militant lawbreakers; an apathy towards the end itself even when it is pursued by the most moderate and conventional means. Here again, however, means change ends: those who use the plea of civilized order as a mask for selfishness or bigotry are doing their part to corrupt civilized order. Their suspected ulterior reasons for opposing questionable means only aggravates the situation that disturbs them, since it is further proof to militants of the corruption they face.

With the tyranny of virtue and the tyranny of the ad hoc goes the tyranny of charisma. Virtue-based attacks on established institutions that claim special privileges of argument or procedure because of crisis conditions or an immoral imbalance of power would frighten off many potential true believers if there were no charismatic leader to embody the cause and dramatize its sanctions with ecstasy, prophecy and miracle. The radical or revolutionary charismatic leader is the surrogate for established order and authority. His tendency is to be functionally infallible since he needs to relieve his followers not only of the burden of the past but of the burden of guilt that might otherwise result from ad hoc procedures.

Since the radical or revolutionary leader stands against a traditional structure, he must in fact free his followers from the necessity of trying to locate themselves in the whole context of time. Time comes to a point in him and so it begins with him; and if his vision is sufficiently apocalyptic it ends with him also. If the past suggests that he is a variation on an ancient delusion, he cancels that past and so is apparently immune from it. He depends on the familiar disjunctions of faith from reason, action from words. It is action that springs from an unquestioning faith that counts; he is sick of words. Though he may need a great number of words to inspire following, he prefers to communicate by demonstration, confrontation, hyperbolic gesture, spontaneous happening, direct violent action. Words delay action, analyze it, qualify it, suggest alternate courses, inevitably lead one back into the past—in short, complicate the issue and overburden faith. In the world of radical charisma (as in the world of American Right Wing politics) complication tends to be a synonym for corruption and the leader is the heroic simplifier (his followers know in their hearts that he is right). This is why he can, in good faith and all honesty, demand the most sweeping and immediate reforms.

It is doubtful if any period in Western civilization has produced more dissident charismatic leaders than the present, or produced them in so many guises: rock poets, underground priests, draft resisters, political revolutionaries, sex athletes, oriental gurus, philosophers, narcotic addicts, astrologers, convicted criminals, actors and television entertainers. Charisma is what occupies the territory that conventional authority is unsure of, can no longer hold or abandons. Charisma liberated from institutional structures is the means men use not only to experience and pursue virtue but to hide from themselves the consequences of an un-

inhibited commitment to those elemental forces
that institutions attempt to domesticate. Hence the
importance of antiestablishment saints, whether
living or dead: Regis Debray, Eldridge Cleaver,
Herbert Marcuse, Norman O. Brown, Franz
Fanon, Che Guevara, Noam Chomsky, Julian and
Judith Beck, Bob Dylan, Albert Camus, Timothy
Leary, Allen Ginsberg, Ken Kesey. They not only
act out their convictions about a new, richer and
more virtuous life but they give comfort and sanction, if not structure, to all those lesser mortals
who would otherwise drift pointlessly or chaotically in the no man's land between their own impulses and organized society. And it is the fear that
they will so pointlessly or chaotically drift that so
often impels men to locate charisma in the most
unlikely subjects—burdening them, sometimes
tragically, with an insistent demand to be led, however violently, to a Promised Land.

The variety of forms in which charisma mani-
fests itself is in relation to the variety of ways in
which established authority has lost, is losing or
is mishandling its sanctions. The charismatic
antiestablishment world therefore defines by caricature the weaknesses and failures of the establishment world. But at the same time it also defines
exactly those threats which the person depends
upon his institutions to defend him against as he
attempts to realize himself in his political, social
and religious capacities.

One of the greatest of these threats is the disjunction between charisma and office or role that is part of the modern bias against the institution. The disjunction is crucial to all strikes against established order as well as to many of the efforts to reform it (of course, established orders may themselves be regularizations of prior disjunctions). To confine charisma to the person and to deny it to the role or office may be psychologically, anthropologically and theologically naive, but it is in effect an immensely simplifying tactic in an immensely complicated world. In the economy of most crusades it is apparently the same kind of indispensable concentration of energy and limitation of attention that, according to British historian H. R. Trevor-Roper, puritanism is in political revolutions.

To separate charisma from role or office in a society of any complexity—in traditional terms, to deny the possibility of structural charisma—is to impose upon it a condition in which it must become less complex, less pluralistic, less tolerant of individual difference, ultimately less tolerant of the person. On the other hand, to limit charisma to a function of institutional role or office—to deny the possibility of nonstructural charisma—is to have the same effect: a sanctified status quo, the embodiment of all virtue, in which the person is always a potential threat. The resemblance of the end results stems from the fact that the charismatic leader, over-determined as he is likely to be by the corruptions of organized society, tends to institutionalize his power with violent ad hoc procedures so that his followers become means (they can be amazingly cooperative) to the establishment of his virtue on a permanent basis. Modern fascist societies have provided giant-size models of this pattern. One of the ironies of the modern scene is the clear fascist potential in so many militants who conceive themselves to be embattled with what is in effect a fascist society.

At the same time, however, some of the most valuable charismatic leaders operate nonstructurally within the institution and aim to reform it in terms of its own announced values. They force it to stretch itself to its limits, even to redefine those limits, particularly the ossifying limitation of charisma to a function of office—which is the religious institution's way of protecting itself against the Holy Spirit. Between their insistent but loving commitment and the simplistic tyranny of "root and branch" enthusiasts there is a crucial difference—a difference that is obscured by the fact that we exist in a world in which those who defend institutions as well as those who attack or attempt to reform them are easily persuaded that they are dispensed persons. The most valuable kind of charismatic leader does not consider himself entitled to special dispensations; in fact, he will probably be aware that the insistence on dispensation is itself a clear sign that the "good" cause has begun its corrupting work.

That corrupting work is the consequence of a kind of intoxication by virtue and charisma. One of the functions of the institutional Church is to protect men from it. *The Legend of the Grand Inquisitor,* in which the Church is organized to protect itself against Christ, parodies this function: for the true function of the Church is to protect Christians from intoxicating limitations of Christ in the interest of making him as available as possible to them in his fullness. Heretics are men who have become intoxicated with such limitations of Christ, to which perhaps prior institutional limitations have disposed them. Having attempted to confine Christ in a narrow context, they are in effect specialists of intense and limited perspective. This is why the heretic's sweet dream of liberation (in the Montanists or Brethren of the Free Spirit, for instance) turns out to be so restricting.

The intoxicant to which the institution easily becomes addicted is of course its own process, in the service of which idol it creates the emergency situations that justify its own ad hoc procedures. Yet it is the institution's commitment to reasoned process that is the hope of the person against the process-destroying tyranny of virtue. Konrad Lorenz' *On Aggression* clarifies the predicament that is engrained in the human condition. On the one hand, says Lorenz, "neither art, nor science, nor indeed any of the great endeavors of humanity would ever have come into being" without the concentrated dedication of militant enthusiasm. On the other hand, militant enthusiasm "is a true autonomous instinct . . . and, like the sexual urge or any other strong instinct, it engenders a specific feeling of strong satisfaction." For Lorenz it is inadequate to explain what I have been calling the tyranny of virtue as simply a reaction to institutional corruption. Men have an innate capacity to create the situations in which they can express militant enthusiasm—which, he points out, is why intelligent men "behave as irrationally and immorally in their political as in their sexual lives." It is also why it may be neither fair nor logical to blame non-violent campaigns against injustice for the riots that often follow in their wake.

Lorenz' book is in agreement with such studies of crowd behavior as Eric Hoffer's *True Believer* and Elias Canetti's *Crowds and Power*, as well as with such a study of the importance of fictions to human living as Frank Kermode's *A Sense of an Ending*. It is a healthy corrective to the long effort in our culture to understand evil purely in terms of the institutional corruption of natural virtue. It also helps to explain a crucial fact about the tyranny of virtue: that it happens to the susceptible. One needs little experience with militant movements to realize how important to them cause-prone personalities are. These are people who have little capacity to serve a substantive cause but a great need of the heightened sense of living that comes from militant cause-serving. The particular cause is little or nothing to them; against the possibility of realizing an announced and specific goal, and so ending the experience of militant enthusiasm, they symbolize and escalate, or they find another cause. If they are not where the action is they supply the action.

Almost of necessity, cause-prone personalities are driven to duplicities as they attempt to keep the trust of more practical confederates: pretending, as Nathan Glazer has observed of the Students for a Democratic Society, to be concerned with substantive issues that are really of only tactical interest to them. Such persons often claim to be aiming at a total revolution in Church or society, which may sound substantive enough. However, total revolution is less a humanly meaningful goal than an expression of the fear of the limiting and even conservative consequences of a specified goal; effectively, it is a battle cry that commits one to nothing but process. Obviously, such people often turn out to be practically useful, if rather hard to manage, in particular "good" causes, and often figure, with some reason, as heroic champions of human liberation. Their charisma lingers long after them, continuing to justify their extra-legal or immoral means, and continuing to hide the once-possible better futures they were instrumental in preventing because they contaminated the ends they professed to serve.

To Lorenz, for whom militant enthusiasm is neither good nor bad in itself, ritual and role are vitally important in keeping a potentially civilizing force from becoming destructive. He writes: "The independent existence of any culture, the creation of a superindividual society that outlives the human being, in other words all that represents true humanity is based on this autonomy of the rite making it an independent motive of human action." To him the austere iconoclast who "regards the pomp of the ritual as an unessential superficiality which even diverts the mind from a deeper absorption in the thing symbolized" is entirely wrong. That deeper absorption in the thing symbolized is an entrancement by the vision of spirit separated from contaminating letter; it can result in a dehumanizing tyranny, for just as man depends on his institutions to protect him from the lusts of virtue, so he depends on the letter to protect him from the lusts of spirit. It can result too, as is apparent enough in these times, in that righteous and militant (and of course honest) inflexibility of mind that sees the roles and rituals of institutional society as simply the means the corrupt establishment uses to maintain itself.

Inflexibility of mind is now, as it has always been, one of the most conspicuous characteristics of the tyranny of virtue. One of its consequences, as John Cogley has pointed out, is that "rudeness, crudity, and blatant, ear-shattering moralism are taken to be the special marks of a journal intent on being honest, outspoken and relevant." They are also the marks of ideological conflict in which persons are expected to subordinate themselves (in all honesty) to grand sanctioning causes in which they become shriller, more simplistic and nonnegotiating in proportion as they engage their opposition. In such a time, as Stephen Spender has said of the passionate ideological polarizations of the Thirties, there is great need "to refute heroic philistines." Yet to press for the definitions, distinctions and rudimentary good manners of civilized discourse in such a time—to insist on the difference between truth-seeking and propaganda or inspired polemic—is to risk being classed as a lukewarm nit-picker or an establishment shill.

The Church is clearly going through such a period. It is quite possible to take the line (as Harvey Cox has, for instance) that God is simply using excessive and radical means to teach the Church a needed lesson (God as cosmic Yippie). The position is by implication a laissez faire one: it may be wrong to oppose the means, but in any event it is futile, for the wave of the future cannot be denied (Cotton Mather and Savonarola had no doubts about the wave of the future).

But at this point in the twentieth century one has sufficient reason to be skeptical of wave-of-the-future arguments: both fascists and communists have demonstrated them to be invitations to cooperate in imposing a strait-jacket on history and human nature. By now Christians should have learned from their own history that the future will always be the product of a dialectic mix of forces, and that one's first duty to whatever group, faction or crusade that claims to be the wave of the future is not to take it at its word but to test it charitably through due process. And the manner of testing is important, for to test it otherwise may be not only to oppose the Holy Spirit but to oppose a possible and highly desirable future.

It is the fear of preventing possible desirable futures that is the negative aspect of what might be called Christian irony. The Christian ironist embodies that combination of flexibility and commitment which characterizes so many of the heroines of Shakespeare's comedies and which is so comically or tragically missing in Shylock, Malvolio, Coriolanus, Othello, Hotspur and Macbeth. In *Man at Play* Hugo Rahner traces his version of this combination to the classic world, and in particular to the virtue that Aristotle calls *eutrapelia*. The *eutrapelos* (literally, "well-turning") man is the happy mean between the frivolous man incapable of commitment and the humorless, and so often zealous, boor who is unaware of options or points of view beyond the one he is fixed in. He has versatility and mobility of soul; he is not trapped "on the hopelessly wrong road of idiotic earnestness, or on the senseless one of exclusive preoccupation with the things of the world."

We have little sympathy with the classic idea of the "mean" and with the Christian theme of gamesome seriousness that Rahner relates to it. Partially because of the nature of classical rhetoric, mean to us suggests compromise; besides, we sense a connection between the notion of the mean and the classic world's suspicion of passion and its emphasis on the general. Our modern conviction is that the person as we know him is somehow involved with a shift of emphasis to the particular and with a relative optimism about passional experience. At its most extreme this conviction sets character formation, and indeed consciousness itself, against the life force and implies an optimistic theology of immoderation: the gods favor with superior insight and an enlarged capacity for life those who heroically commit themselves to impulse. So we have our dreams of a global village in which the long aberrations of rational consciousness will have been corrected by the gut bonds of the shamanistic and narcoticized tribe: and in which, of course, the person as we know him will have disappeared.

Our own century has made it clear how favorable such a climate is to the development of tyrants of virtue and ad hoc morality. Inevitably they are responded to, in the Church and in society generally, with backlash emphases on law and order that are caricatures of vital institutional order. Involved everywhere in this extreme dialectic of immoderation and backlash is that painful and characteristic experience of the modern person: his repeated discovery of the illusion of all he had been induced to hope for. In such a time the cynical refusal to commit oneself to any cause or any transcendent value is itself a form of protective backlash.

This protective cynicism (which in modern literature removes both the joy and critical bite from comedy and makes tragedy impossible) is a caricature of the *eutrapelia* that is for Father Rahner "the forgotten virtue." His *eutrapelos* man, being informed with Christian irony and a sense of play, is, negatively considered, spared the agonies that come from the misplaced hopes and restricted perspectives of "idiotic earnestness." Positively considered, however, he is the committed man who honors his commitments with the flexibility of mind and soul that comes from the awareness of other options and the possibility (because of the limitations of any given moment in time) of larger perspectives. Like the ideal man implied by Lorenz' book, he knows that without a sense of play, expressing itself in ritual and ceremonial as well as in games, humanity would be devastated by its own vital energies and monstrified by its virtues.

Such an ironist can be described, as Rahner describes his *homo vere ludens,* as "the man who is at the exact midpoint between heaven and earth," who can conceive of his life and all the events of his world as "a great theatrical performance, for he knows something of the secret that is behind the stage." With this special knowledge, ". . . he can do without agonizing over the state of the world or greedily devouring the things it has to offer."

The play metaphor here (it is also central to Shakepeare's vision of the world) can be misleading, since it is a structural metaphor not only for a Stoic and Christian contempt of the world but for a familiar modern despair that follows on the realization that one has misplaced his faith or the discovery that there are too many conflicting positions of faith. No doubt there have been times in Western civilization when a Stoic or Christian detachment was the only available instrument of survival for some men and women; certainly it has been bound up with important cultural achievements. But whatever personal agonies or confusions it has in the past tended to make more bearable, it is too easy and too inflexible for the Christian now; it implies an attachment to too simple a future and depends for its clarity upon a crippling avoidance of too much relevant information—resembling in these respects the condition that exists under the tyranny of virtue.

The position of the Christian ironist is as difficult as that of Rahner's *homo vere ludens:* he lives in a dialectic tension between two worlds as if he were walking a tightrope. He must commit himself in the awareness of perspectives beyond his commitment and of the partiality of his knowledge; he must act knowing that the future he aims at is not likely to be the one taking shape in the womb of time; that even if his action is successful its very success will create unanticipated problems, so that there may be little if any gain; that he may discover himself ultimately to have been the agent of change that is only progress from a point of view that change itself has made untenable. Most importantly, he will involve himself generously in the continuing effort of renewal that Christianity should be knowing that at every moment that effort is bound to fail in some measure and that every failure is a point of fresh beginning.

The psychiatrist Kenneth Keniston, speaking of the "moral precocity" of youth in the September-October, 1969, *Critic*, has pointed out that intense moral passion may exist "in the absence of a developed capacity for compassion, empathy and love for one's fellow men." The passionate search for moral purity which characterizes so many failed revolutions suggests to him "that the combination of abstract principles with a humorless and loveless asceticism is especially likely to be dangerous." The Christian ironist will stand against this combination because he has a vision of human potential that is neither utopian nor pessimistic but charitable. Charity in action, as St. Paul defines it, is ironic; it is the Christian's intellectual and spiritual toughness in the face of the cross-purposes, internal contradictions, multiple perspectives and unanticipated consequences that result as much from the time-bound mysteriousness of man's environment as from his perversity and short-sightedness. Without charity men make themselves mad attempting to drive life into a corner where it can be caught in one grand terminal formula that in effect stops time. And time in the end is what the tyrant of virtue uncharitably and without irony lusts against.